It's About Time!

by Stuart J. Murphy · **illustrated by John Speirs**

HarperCollins*Publishers*

To Justin, whose hours and days
are filled with joy
—S.J.M.

For Brody, Gemma, and Dennis
—J.S.

The publisher and author would like to thank teachers Patricia Chase,
Phyllis Goldman, and Patrick Hopfensperger for their help
in making the math in MathStart just right for kids.

HarperCollins®, ■®, and MathStart® are registered trademarks of
HarperCollins Publishers. For more information about the MathStart series,
write to HarperCollins Children's Books, 1350 Avenue of the Americas,
New York, NY 10019, or visit our website at www.mathstartbooks.com.

Bugs incorporated in the MathStart series design were painted by Jon Buller.

It's About Time!
Text copyright © 2005 by Stuart J. Murphy
Illustrations copyright © 2005 by John Speirs
Manufactured in China by South China Printing Company Ltd.

Library of Congress Cataloging-in-Publication Data
Murphy, Stuart J.
  It's about time! / by Stuart J. Murphy ; illustrated by John Speirs.— 1st ed.
p. cm. — (MathStart)
ISBN 0-06-055768-0 — ISBN 0-06-055769-9 (pbk.)
1. Time—Juvenile literature. [1. Time. 2. Day. 3. Night.] I. Speirs, John, ill.
II. Title. III. Series.
QB209.5.M87 2005   2003027524
529—dc22

Typography by Elynn Cohen   2 3 4 5 6 7 8 9 10   ❖ First Edition

Be sure to look for all of these **MathStart** books!

7:00 A.M.

Wake-up time—a great big stretch.

4

8:00 A.M.

Time for school—hurry up!

Time to learn and time to play.

9:00 A.M.

Time with all my friends.

Now it's time to go back home.

Noontime now. "It's time for lunch."

Story time—my favorite time.

10

Then, for me, it's quiet time.

Soon it's time to jump and run.

3:00 P.M.

Time to swing up high.

13

Help-out time—I do my best.

5:00 P.M.

14

Dinnertime—oh, yuck. It's peas!

Bath time now—but I'm not dirty!

7:00 P.M.

Bedtime next—but I'm not sleepy!

8:00 P.M.

The lights go out. It's dark in here!

9:00 P.M.

Scary shadows creep.

A monster friend would keep me safe.

11:00 P.M.

It's midnight now—and here he is!

My monster brought a lot of friends.

1:00 A.M.

"Party time!" they shout.

2:00 A.M.

Clap and dance, twirl and swing.

3:00 A.M.

Climb and jump—fall and crash!

25

It's about time you went away!

26

Now it's comfy, cozy time.

Wake-up time—a great big stretch.

7:00 A.M.

28

Time to start another day.

7:00 A.M.

8:00 A.M.

9:00 A.M.

10:00 A.M.

3:00 P.M.

4:00 P.M.

5:00 P.M.

6:00 P.M.

11:00 P.M.

12:00

1:00 A.M.

2:00 A.M.

In *It's About Time!*, the math concept is telling time. Reading both digital and analog (or traditional) clock faces is an important part of everyday life. The first steps in mastering this skill are learning to tell time to the nearest hour and gaining an understanding of elapsed time.

If you would like to have more fun with the math concepts presented in *It's About Time!*, here are a few suggestions:

- Explain to the child that a day has 24 hours. The hours from 12:00 midnight to 12:00 noon are called A.M. hours. The hours from 12:00 noon to 12:00 midnight are called P.M. hours. Noon and midnight are neither A.M. nor P.M.

- Before rereading the story, show the child an analog and a digital clock and explain that analog clocks have hands on the clock face while digital clocks show time using just numbers. Then look for different types of clocks around the house.

- As you read the story with the child, have an analog clock available so that the child can move the hands on the clock face to correspond to the times in the story.

- Have the child draw clocks with hands that show the time that he or she gets up, goes to school, eats dinner, and goes to bed. Write the digital time alongside each clock.

- Tell the child a time (for example, 5:00), and ask the child what time it will be one hour from then, or what time was it one hour before.

Following are some activities that will help you extend the concepts presented in *It's About Time!* into a child's everyday life:

Picture the Time: Have the child draw a picture of him- or herself doing various activities at different times of the day. Help him or her write the time on each picture.

TV Time: Use the TV schedule from a newspaper and have the child find his or her favorite shows. Talk about what time each show begins and ends.

What Time Is It?: Describe a particular activity (such as lunchtime or nap time) and have the child tell you what time it would start. If correct, he or she can pick the next activity and you be the one to say what time it would occur.

Clock Collage: Find pictures in magazines that show different clocks and different times. Make a collage of the pictures. Have the child circle each clock that shows the time on the hour.

The following books include some of the same concepts that are presented in *It's About Time!*:

• CLOCKS AND MORE CLOCKS by Pat Hutchins

• MY FIRST BOOK OF TIME by Claire Llewellyn

• TRAIN LEAVES THE STATION by Eve Merriam